AF476922

First published in Great Britain 1984 by
Webb and Bower (Publishers) Limited
9 Colleton Crescent, Exeter, Devon EX2 4BY

Edited, designed and illustrated by
the E.T. Archive Limited
Chelsea Wharf, 15 Lots Road, London SW10 0QH

Designed by Julian Holland
Picture Research by Anne-Marie Ehrlich
Special photography by Eileen Tweedy
Copyright © text and illustrations E.T. Archive Ltd 1984

British Library Cataloguing in Publication Data

Gordon, Lesley
  The language of flowers.—(A Webb & Bower miniature)
  1. Symbolism of flowers—Pictorial works
  I. Title
  398′.368213′0222   GR780

  ISBN 0–86350–017–X

Phototypset by Text Filmsetters Limited, Orpington, Kent
Printed and bound in Hong Kong by Mandarin Offset International Limited

THE LANGUAGE OF FLOWERS

Lesley Gordon

Webb & Bower
EXETER, ENGLAND

The Language of Flowers

The language of flowers is said to be as old as the world, but we must believe that love filled the heart before the hand could fashion hieroglyphics. The Chinese were thought to have retained an ancient alphabet composed entirely of plants and roots, which is possible to believe from looking at modern Chinese script. During the violence of the French Revolution, Roucher, a political prisoner, studied floral language, and his daughter was allowed to send flowers to the prison for him. A few days before he died on the scaffold, he sent her two dried lilies, as a sign of the purity of his heart and the fate that awaited him.

When in the Victorian era the language of flowers became a romantic fashion, it was no easy task to become a fluent linguist. To avoid misunderstanding and consequent embarrassment, it was necessary to learn the exact manner in which a posy, or a single flower, should be offered. A pansy held upright denoted heart's ease; reversed, it would indicate the heart disturbed. Cupid, they say, is blind, but at these delicate moments he needed to keep his eyes open.

The dimensions of this miniature language of flowers indicate that love must be kept to a similar scale. One must learn to walk in flowery meadows before one can run, but it was Byron, that experienced lover, who swore

> By all those token flowers that tell
> What words can never speak so well.

Carnation

Dianthus caryophyllus   Affection

The generic name *Dianthus* means Jove's flower. Coronations or carnations as they became, were so named from their use in the crowns and garlands worn by successful lovers. Later, in Gerard's time, they were popularly known as tuggies, after Mistress Tuggie of Westminster, who had a wonderful collection of them. Language of flowers purists give different meanings to eight carnations.

Yellow	*Disdain*
Yellow-pink	*Disdain and rejection*
White-pink	*Refusal and departure*
Red-pink	*Lively and pure love*
Striped-pink	*Refusal*
White	*A woman's love*
Deep red	*Alas, for my poor heart*
Striped-red	*Extremes*

The carnation is almost the oldest garden-flower, and one of the most cared for. Pliny claimed that it was discovered in Spain in the time of Augustus Caesar. The Spaniards used it in beverages for its clove flavour, which later led to its old English name of sops-in-wine. William Cobbett wrote enthusiastically 'for my part, as a thing to keep, and not to sell; as a thing, the possession of which is to give me pleasure, I hesitate not a moment to prefer the plant of a fine Carnation to a gold watch set with diamonds'.

Carnation
Fascination

Convolvulus

Convolvulus   Fleeting Joys

Though no favourite of farmers or gardeners, the wild convolvulus or bindweed is even more beautiful than the cultivated varieties. The pink- and white-striped lesser bindweed, *C. arvensis*, is a charming shepherdess among fields, but the pure-white trumpet of the greater bindweed, *C. sepium*, not only decorates hedges, but often recklessly climbs telegraph poles, a feat no one could have anticipated.

An old anonymous herbalist said of the greater bindweed, 'there is an herbe named, in Latine, Convolvulus, growing among shrubs and bushes, which carrieth a floure not unlike to the Lily, saveth that it yieldeth no smell. For whitenesse they resemble one another very much, as if nature, in making this floure, were a-learning, and trying her skill how to frame the Lily indeed.' Sadly, this lovely countryside pattern of the lily is a strangler, whose penetrating roots exhaust the soil and can seldom be exterminated. Its specific name, *sepium*, comes from the Latin, *sepes*, a hedge, and it has been made the emblem of dangerous insinuation. Lesser bindweed is the symbol of obstinacy. The dwarf convolvulus of our gardens, *C. minor tricolor*, whose flowers are a bright combination of blue, yellow and white, was given the sentiment of Love Levels All.

Some of the climbing varieties of convolvulus twine from right to left, and no stern measures can persuade them to do otherwise. They must abide by their instincts or die.

Cypress

Cupressus   Mourning

The cypress is regarded as the funeral tree of the eastern world, and is therefore dedicated to the dead. It takes its name from Cyparissus, son of Telephus of Cea, who was loved by Apollo. Having accidentally killed his friend's favourite stag, Cyparissus died of grief, and was changed by Apollo into a cypress tree.

> Henceforth, when mourners grieve, their grief to
>   share,
> Emblem of woe, the cypress shall be there.

The shade of the tree and its fragrance was believed to be deadly by the Greeks and Romans. Gerard said that it had been dedicated to Pluto, 'whereupon it is thought that the shadow thereof is unfortunate'. He also noted that 'Theophrastus attributeth great honour to this tree, shewing that the roots of Old Temples became famous by reason of that wood, and that the timber thereof, of which the rafters are made is everlasting, and it is not hurt there by rotting, cobweb, nor any other infirmitie or corruption'.

In Turkey the upright cypress was planted at graves, to indicate the ascension of the soul to heaven. Shakespeare associated a grove of cypress trees with murdering basilisk, lizards, stings, poison and gall, 'and all the foul terrors in dark-seated hell'. *King Henry VI, Part 2*, III. ii.

Combined with the marigold, Inquietude, the two have been made the emblem of despair.

Dahlia

Dahlia variabiles

Pomp

The dahlia is a native of Mexico, where it is found in sandy meadows, growing several hundred feet above sea-level. It was brought to England in 1789, neglected and lost, and it was not until 1804 that Professor Andrew Dahl, a Swedish botanist after whom it was called, presented it to Lady Holland, who became its first successful English cultivator. Its thick stems, coarse leaves, crude colouring and lack of perfume have prevented it from becoming warmly welcomed, although it is popular as a bedding plant in public parks. There is a touch of the *nouveau riche* about it which cannot be ignored and has evidently led to its being made the symbol of pomp in the language of flowers. More appreciative flower linguists have given it a typically Victorian and involved sentiment, My Gratitude Exceeds Your Care, which might well leave the recipient mystified.

The dahlia needs little attention after planting, but it cannot be ignored that the first frost reduces it to an unsavoury blackened heap and the cleaning and winter storage of the tubers is no light matter.

There is little folklore attached to its history, but in medicine the dahlia comes into its own. The tubers contain a kind of insulin known as dahlin, which, in the form of diabetic sugar, is prescribed for diabetic and consumptive patients. It was used in World War II as a much-needed drug for the army. It was not until 1929 that it was discovered in America that dahlia tubers had been used medicinally for centuries in Mexico.

The Dahlia
Dahlia
Instability

Daisy

Bellis perennis   Innocence

The daisy's ancient name of Herb Margaret had almost disappeared by the end of the nineteenth century and it may still be seen in old herbals as bairnswort, the child's flower, or bruisewort, a remedy for bruises. Daisy roots were once believed to stunt growth, and boiled in milk they were frequently given to puppies to keep them small. The roots – and cream – were also administered by fairy godmothers of old to the lanky. They were much valued by the lovelorn. Those who wished to have pleasant dreams of the loved and absent put daisy roots under their pillow, or if they pulled up a handful of grass with their eyes shut, the number of daisies it contained forecast their number of unmarried years.

Some years ago, Robin Lane Fox wrote an article on the decline of the daisy, in which he said, 'the daisy's disgrace is complete. Her reward is a fortnightly dose of poison, her death a growth industry for chemicals and machines.' Wordsworth knew better than that. He wrote of her as 'A little Cyclops with one eye, Staring to threaten and defy', and if statisticians were employed in the pleasant occupation of counting daisy heads on any given sunny summer day, it seems certain that it would be Robin Lane Fox instead of the daisy who would suffer defeat.

In Christian art, the daisy may often be seen clasped in the hand of the Infant Jesus as a symbol of innocence. In the language of flowers it is the emblem of gentleness.

Aufyne
Dayes

Forget-Me-Not

The botanical name of the forget-me-not, *Myosotis*, means mouse-ear, in reference to the shape of its leaves. All the species were once called scorpion grass, because the curled flower-heads were thought to resemble a scorpion's tail, and were therefore expected to cure a scorpion's sting. Gerard said that the leaves 'boyled in wine and drunke, prevaile against the said bitings, as also of addars, snakes, and such venomous beasts'.

Today the forget-me-not is regarded as a fashionable favourite of the nineteenth century, which has sadly become a trifle démodé. In those days it was embossed on valentines, painted on china, lithographed on scraps and ornamental texts, embroidered on slippers, smoking-jackets and caps, and painstakingly reproduced by young ladies in albums. It headed notepaper and menus, and was top favourite on birthday cards, and its gold-eyed pink and blue flowers, cunningly reproduced in velvet, adorned ladies' bonnets and children's hats. By the middle of the century they were sold in bunches or in pots in the Paris markets, and they were also planted by the Germans around their graves – a homely way of say 'Lest we forget'.

Francis Kilvert wrote in his diary of finding a silk bookmarker with 'Forget-Me-Not' embroidered on it. It was a gift from a childhood sweetheart. But from which one? 'I gazed at the words conscience-stricken. Forget-Me-Not. And I had forgotten.'

Reserve thy smiles
for me

Geranium

Geranium   Stupidity

This plant is divided into three genera – *Erodium*, the heron's-bill, *Pelargonium*, the stork's-bill, and *Geranium*, the crane's-bill. The name geranium is derived from the Greek, and signifies a crane, the fruit resembling a crane's bill. It was used to staunch blood of green wounds when bruised and applied, and a decoction cured ulcers and ulcerated throats.

Each of the many varieties of geranium is given a different meaning in the language of flowers.

Wild geranium (Herb Robert)	*Steadfast piety*
Ivy geranium	*Bridal favour*
Lemon geranium	*Unexpected meeting*
Oak-leaved geranium	*True friendship*
Pencilled geranium	*Ingenuity*
Silver-leaved geranium	*Recall*
Rose-scented geranium	*Preference*

The soft-scented leaves of the rose-scented geranium seem to offer themselves to be rubbed, much as a kitten loves to be stroked. The unfortunate common scarlet geranium owes its adoption as the emblem of stupidity to Madame de Staël, who after suffering a boring conversation with a handsome young Swiss officer in full regimentals, peevishly likened him to a scarlet geranium – a fine colour, but lacking an acceptable perfume.

Holly

Ilex

Foresight

The holly was once a popular divination plant to be consulted on Christmas eve. Tiny pieces of candle were put on the leaves and floated in water. They were then lit, and according to whether they floated or sank, the success or failure of one's affairs could be predicted. Holly was also used to test the fidelity of the absent lover. In the north of England, three holly leaves to which names were given were put under the pillow with the left hand, and the blessing of the Trinity was invoked. The first leaf to turn by morning represented the future husband or wife. Cattle will thrive and sheep produce twins if holly is fastened up where they can see it on Christmas Eve, that they too may rejoice on the anniversary of Christ's birth.

The holly was made the emblem of foresight, because Nature protects it with thorny leaves until it has grown above the reach of cattle, after which it continues to a considerable height without prickles.

During the festival of Saturnalia which occurred at about the same time as Christmas, the Romans would send holly boughs to their friends with their greetings, and so it was also given the sentiment of good wishes.

There is one holly superstition that is still in common practice – holly and all other Christmas decorations must be taken down on Candlemas Eve.

Honeysuckle

The botanical name of *Lonicera* was given to the honeysuckle by Linnaeus in honour of Adam Lonicer, a German botanist of the sixteenth century. To country people it was known as woodbine or woodbind, suckling and caprifoly, meaning goat-leaf, since it was believed to be the favourite food of goats. In the language of flowers several variations of its meaning can be found – devotion and affection, generosity and gaiety, and rustic beauty.

Villagers used the juice of its leaves to ease the pain of bee-stings, but it was also written in an old treatise on herbs that 'if the bee-hive be anoynted with the juyce of the leeves, the been schalt not goo away: the housbondes kept his swarmes in tyme of yere by such anoyntynge'. Culpeper offers very little help on the subject. 'It is a plant so common, that everyone that hath eyes knows it, and he that hath none, cannot read a description, if I should write it.'

Its windings follow the sun from east to west. Insects make their way to the base of the tubes in search of honey, and sometimes find it easier to emerge by eating their way out than by climbing back, so leaving small exit holes by way of acknowledgement.

The good conservationist John Parkinson wrote in 1629, 'the Honisuckle that groweth wylde in every hedge, although it be very sweete yet doe I not bring into my garden, but let it rest in his owne place to serve their sens that travell by it, or have no garden'.

Lonicera Periclymenum.

Lilac

Syringa vulgaris   First Emotions of Love

The lilac, in spite of its connections with China, Persia and the mountainous regions of northern Europe, has settled down happily in the English garden, and stays, like the robin, as near to the house as it is allowed. Kipling called it the Doorway Lilac. It was introduced into Britain during the reign of Henry VIII, and although thoroughly domesticated in these days, its story is full of argument and superstition. The argument arose from a complicated confusion of names, whereby the flower we know as syringa is really *Philadelphus*, and the flower we know as lilac is really *Syringa*. Gerard called the purple lilac, 'Syringa, the blew Pipe Tree, because its stems, when the pith is removed, are hollow like a pipe's'; and the *Philadelphus*, he called the White Pipe Tree, thereby causing a misunderstanding that three hundred years has scarcely settled.

The superstitions are equally confusing. 'If a lilac is chopped down over the Welsh border, other lilacs will mourn its loss, and refuse to bloom the following year.' 'It is unlucky to bring lilac, especially white lilac, into the house.' 'It is a flower of death and presages misfortune; and is often laid in coffins.' 'Should a lover offer lilac to his fiancée, the engagement will be broken off.' All this is what 'they' say – but forget it. Why not remember instead, that the lilac marks the beginning of summer and of love.

RIMMEL'S
ALMANACK
LILAC.
MARCH.
APRIL.
FIRST LOVE
Sweet harbinger of Spring, we welcome with rapture
Thy verdant boughs teeming with perfumes of the south
Thou unbosom'st to us the first charms of Nature
A pure and fresh emblem of the first love of youth.

Lily

The Madonna lily, dedicated to St Anthony, protector of marriages, is one of the most ancient of cultivated flowers. It may be seen in a tenth-century miniature in the Benedictional of Saint Ethelwold of Winchester. It shares honours with the rose of symbolizing the Immaculate Conception, and was the crusading device of the heraldic arms of the Virgin. It was grown by the Romans, who called it *Candidum*, and it is believed to have been transported across Europe by the Roman legions.

Folklore accumulates round such an ancient and lovely flower, which was said to arise from the grave of one who had been unjustly executed, as a token of his innocence. For a man to step on a lily means the loss of purity of the women in his household. Women maintained that the Madonna lily will grow only for a good woman, or where the mistress is master – not necessarily the same thing. Another regional saying holds that when Madonna lilies are prolific, bread will be cheap that year. To dream of lilies brings good luck.

Lilies were planted in monastery gardens, not only for their beauty and for their religious significance, but for very practical medicinal purposes. Godorus, serjeant-surgeon to Queen Elizabeth I, is said to have cured many people of dropsy using the juice of lily roots mixed with barley flour baked in cakes, and eaten with meat instead of bread.

Lily of the Valley

Convalleria is variously named by country people as conval lily or lily convally, lilly constancy, and even better, liriconfancie; Lady's tears or Mary's tears, from the tears that Mary shed at the foot of the Cross; May lily, and ladder-to-heaven, a name probably given by medieval monks from the step-like arrangement of the perfumed bells. In Devon it was considered unlucky to plant a bed of lilies of the valley, as the person who did so would probably die within the year. It was also unlucky to bring them into the house, or to give them to a friend.

Baskets of lilies of the valley were once brought into towns for sale during their short season, and lily picnics, known as lily-pics, were arranged in suitable parts of the country. Happiness it certainly brought, but its alternative meaning is unconscious sweetness.

This unassuming flower, a scented pearl, as Alphonse Karr in 1859 called it, has an unexpectedly bloodthirsty legend connected with it. In the Sussex woods near Horsham, a tremendous battle was fought between St Leonard and a fiery dragon. After mortal combat lasting many hours the beast was finally vanquished, leaving the woodland freely spattered with the saint's blood. Wherever the blood fell, lilies of the valley sprang up to commemorate the saint's desperate fight against evil, and the woods, now called St Leonard's Forest, are still thickly carpeted with lilies bearing witness to the truth of the tale.

Marguerite

Chrysanthemum leucanthemum   Obstacle

The generic name of the ox-eye daisy or marguerite comes from the Greek, *chrysos*, gold and *anthos*, flower. The specific name is also from the Greek, and signifies a white flower. In some parts of Somerset it was called the dun-daisy, from a supposed connection with Thor, the god of thunder. In Scotland and the north of England it was known as the gowan, golding or gool. Its presence was known to be an indication of poor soil, and in Scotland 'gool-ridings' were established for the purpose of exterminating this weed from the cornfields. Farmers whose fields were found so neglected as to produce a large crop of gools had to pay the penalty of a wether sheep. The custom is supposed to have originated with the Vice-Chancellor of Henry VI, who established the gool-ridings in order to punish the farmers on his land for their negligence in not ridding the corn of the 'carr-gulds'. In Denmark and Saxony the gulds also grew within reach of the law.

Dedicated to Artemis, the goddess of nature and fertility, the ox-eye daisy was used to cure women's complaints. It is employed as a tonic, and for whooping cough and asthma, and country people formerly made a concoction of the fresh plant in ale, as a cure for jaundice.

It was dedicated by Christians to Mary Magdalene, and was known to Gerard as maudlin-wort. The language of flowers also makes it symbolic of patience.

ad compleroium.
onuerte nos deus
salutaris n̄r et aue
te nā tuā a nobis

Orange Blossom

The brides of the ancient Saracens wore orange blossom at their weddings as an emblem of fecundity – since an average sized orange tree can yield four thousand oranges in a single year! Although the same emblem has been worn by European brides ever since the Crusades, it was not until the introduction of the language of flowers by the Victorian modistes and its more modest symbolism of chastity that orange blossom met with such wide approval by brides and their mamas. Wreaths of orange blossom could be worn only by virgin brides, and a fashion book of 1869 warned, 'this decoration is withheld from all who are undeserving of the distinction, more especially in the neighbourhood of Paris', which may well be the reason why orange blossom has gone out of fashion. Before the custom petered out altogether, however, it was followed by the wearing of the bridal bonnet, trimmed with artificial orange blossom sprays, a short-lived fashion although it must have enhanced the desirability of almost any bride. At the time 'to gather orange blossoms' meant to seek for a wife.

Alluding to the orange tree's habit of producing flowers and fruit simultaneously, Tom Moore (1779-1852) wrote,

> Just then, beneath some orange trees,
> Whose fruit and blossoms in the breeze
> Were wantoning together, free,
> Like age at play with infancy...

Pansy

  Thoughts

The numerous large velvety garden pansies bred today are descended from two British wild species, *V. tricolor*, the three-coloured heart's-ease, and *V. lutea*, the yellow mountain pansy, both happily still with us. It is, however, the little heart's-ease that is the most appealing, and the source of so many of its ridiculous names, such as Johnny-jump-up, three-faces-in-a-hood, kiss-me-at-the-garden-gate, and, of course, Shakespeare's name, love-in-idleness.

Thomas Miller, in his *Language of Flowers or the Pilgrimage of Love*, published in about 1847 and dedicated to the Rosebud of England, the Princess Royal, invented an ingenious form of divination depending on the lines on pansies' faces.

If the petal plucked was pencilled with four lines, it
signified hope; if the centre line started a branch, when
the streaks numbered five, it was still hope, springing
out of fear; and when the lines were thickly branched,
and leaned towards the left, they foretold a life of trouble;
but if they bent towards the right, they were then
supposed to denote prosperity unto the end: seven
streaks they interpreted into constancy in love, and if the
centre one was longest, they prophesied that Sunday
would be their wedding-day; eight denoted fickleness;
nine, a changing heart; and eleven – the most ominous
number of all – disappointment in love and an early grave.

Spūs scī sup[er] q[uem] ... coluba baptisa. mathei 3
Ad primam Vo
Eus in adiutorii me
ii intende Die ad ro
iu adiui me festina

Passion Flower

Passiflora

Christian Faith

On first sight, these wonderful flowers, larger, more colourful and far more fragrant in the dense forests of South America than most Europeans can imagine, appeared to the invading Spanish as a God-given symbol of Christ's Passion, and therefore a means of converting the natives of Mexico to the Christian faith. The leaf of the maracoc, as it was called, represented a spear and the five anthers of the flowers symbolized the Five Wounds. The missionaries likened the tendrils to the cords and whips and the column of the ovary to the pillar of the Cross. The stamens recalled the hammers, and the dramatic dark circle of thread of the corona, the crown of thorns. Its name, maracoc or maracuia, was changed to *Flor de los Cinco Llagas*, Flower of the Five Wounds, later to be condensed by Linnaeus into *Passiflora*, the Passion flower. Today the Japanese know it as the clock flower, because from sunrise to sunset the flowers turn clockwise.

The fruit of certain edible species yields a drug that is used in homeopathic medicine for the treatment of epilepsy.

According to the religious persuasion of the editors of the language of flowers, *Passiflora* is either the emblem of Christian faith, or the symbol of religious superstition.

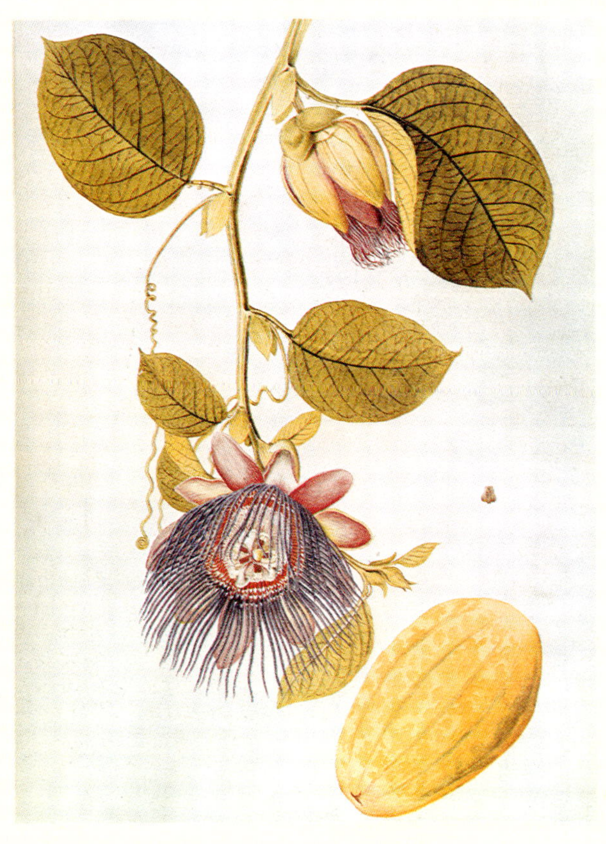

Pink

The ultimate in tidiness and prettiness. We speak of 'the pink of perfection', though we seldom meet with it.

> And 'clipping pinks' (which maiden's Sunday gowns
> Full often wear catcht at by toying chaps)
> Pink as the ribbons round their snowy caps.
>
> *John Clare, The Shepherd's Calender, 1827*

The growing of painted ladies and the old laced pinks of cottage gardens became the spare-time hobby of the miners of Durham and Northumberland, and of the small band of craftsmen near Glasgow, the Paisley weavers, for whom the flower has become almost a symbol.

The pink is a native of eastern Europe, and a later arrival in Britain than the carnation. It was found naturalized on the walls of Beaulieu Abbey, where it may have grown from the days of the Cistercian monks. The best known of all cottage-garden pinks is 'Mrs Sinkins', whose name seems as fringed as its petals. It was raised in a workhouse garden by the Master of Slough Poor Law Institution, and named after his wife. When Slough became a borough in 1938, this proud pink was incorporated in its coat of arms.

A writer in a nineteenth-century magazine gives a magnificent picture of the manner in which he cultivated pinks by putting them into ivory boxes, with their stems fastened to black wands by means of silver rings.

Primrose

Primula   Young Love

The primrose derived its name from *primus*, since it is one of the earliest spring flowers. Chaucer called it the Primerole. It was anciently known as Paralysos, after a beautiful youth, son of Priapus and Flora, who died of grief for the loss of his betrothed, Melicenta. His parents preserved his memory in the annual appearance of the frail flowers of the primrose.

Gerard advises those who feel a 'phrensie' coming on to take a few drops of primrose tea. 'Take the leaves and floures of Primrose, boile them a little in fountaine water, and in some rose and Betony waters, adding thereto sugar, pepper, salt and butter, which being strained, to drink first and last.' Country people made of its leaves and flowers a pale yellow salve called spring salve. Culpeper also made a primrose salve; 'Of the leaves of Primroses is made as fine a salve to heal wounds as any that I know; you shall be taught to make salves of any herb at the latter end of the book: make this as you are taught there and do not (you that have any ingenuity in you) see your poor neighbours go with wounded limbs when an halfpenny cost will heal them.'

So far the primrose has been regarded as a useful plant, for kitchen and stillroom only, but Izaak Walton saw it in a different light. 'When I sat last on this primrose bank, and looked down on the meadows, I thought of them, as Charles the Emperor did of Florence, that they were too pleasant to be looked on, but only on holidays.'

Thistle

Carduus   Independence

The thistle is the national emblem of Scotland and is of ancient and honourable ancestry. Its motto, *Nemo me impune lacessit*, familiarly known to the Scots as 'Wha daur meddle wi' me?' refers to the wars with Denmark. A marauding Danish army, intending to surprise a Scottish camp by night, advanced barefoot upon the sleeping men, when a soldier, stepping on a thistle, gave a cry of pain. At this, the Scottish camp suddenly awakened, leapt to its defence, and defeated the invaders, and the 'guardian thistle' was taken as their emblem.

About 1824 Henry Phillips wrote, 'It is now so happily blended with the English rose, that we hope no hand will escape the prickles of each, who shall dare to divide them'.

In spite of its sentiments of austerity, sternness, and independence, the thistle has also a reputation for cheerfulness, which it owes perhaps to Dioscorides, who claimed that 'the root borne about one...removes all diseases of melancholy'. Culpeper admitted that 'their virtues are but few, but these are not to be despised; for the decoction of the thistle in wine being drank, expels superfluous melancholy out of the body, and makes a man as merry as a cricket'.

The delicately cut paper leaves in this valentine reveal, when lifted, three sentiments more platonic than patriotic. They are courage, sincerity and friendship.

A token of regard.
For Auld
Lang Syne

Vine

The vine was dedicated to Dionysus, the youthful and beautiful god of wine. He was also known as Bacchus, by both Greeks and Romans. It was said that the vine bore three kinds of fruit – intoxication, voluptuousness and repentance. As the cultivation of the vine spread in Greece, the worship of Dionysus likewise spread further, and the celebration of the Bacchic festivals became more and more dissolute and wild.

In the Bible the vine combined with the fig to become the embodiment of peace, relaxation and well-being. 'They shall sit every man under his vine and under his fig-tree, and none shall make them afraid.' Micah iv. 4. Although the Greeks worshipped Dionysus and the Egyptians, Osiris, as the god of wine, it was Christian belief that Noah planted the first vineyard when he stepped on to dry land, and therefore it is to Noah that we owe, not only the pleasures of wine, but also the dried fruits, currants, sultanas and raisins, which are such valuable additions to our diet.

The timber of the grapevine is of enormous strength and may reach a great age. Pliny, who died in the eruption of Vesuvius in AD 79 wrote that he knew of one that was already six hundred years old. Although it has been given the sentiment of intoxication in the language of flowers, it is known, more circumspectly, as the emblem of fruitfulness.

Willow

Salix   Melancholy

The willow family consists of three genera, the two better-known being *Salix* and *Populus*, and Richard St Barbe Baker claimed recently that it was the poplar and not the willow on which the Jews hung their harps during their captivity.

> By the rivers of Babylon, there we sat down, yea, we wept, when we remembered Zion. We hanged our harps upon the willows in the midst thereof. For there they that carried us away required of us a song; and they that wasted us required of us mirth . . . .
>
> *Psalm 137, 1-3*

From this ancient time the weeping willow, *S. babylonica*, has been regarded as the true emblem of melancholy. A common refrain of sixteenth century lovers was

> All a green willow, willow, willow,
> All a green willow is my garland,

but Shakespeare most of all moves us with a mere weeping tree in *Othello* when Desdemona recalls

> My mother had a maid called Barbara,
> She was in love, and he she lov'd prov'd mad
> And did forsake her; she had a song of 'willow';
> An old thing 'twas, but it expressed her fortune,
> And she died singing it.

Sources and Acknowledgements